A Mother's Prayer And God's Miraculous Answer

By
Korene Sturtz

A Mother's Prayer
And God's Miraculous Answer
Copyright © 2015 by Korene Sturtz

The views expressed in this book do not necessarily reflect those of the publisher.

eBook: 978-1-312-90931-1

Paperback: 978-1-312-90927-4

Hardcover: 978-1-312-90930-4

Worldwide Publishing Group

Your multi-platform publishing partner

7710-T Cherry Park Drive, Suite 224, Houston, Texas 77095

www.WorldwidePublishingGroup.com

(713) 766-4272

Thank you for your purchase. A portion of the proceeds from the sales of this book is donated to "The Sturtz Boys' GSD Fund". This fund helps support the work of Dr. Davd Weinstein and the Glycogen Storage Disease Research Department at the University of Florida.

Table of Contents

INTRODUCTION

My story is told to give hope to everyone who needs a miracle. I encourage you to persevere through your trials and tests. We have to change our perspective, look beyond our circumstances, and step into the promises the Lord has made to us.

As I write this, my wonderful husband Darin and I have been married for twenty years and have five children: Aubriana, Madison, Cameron, Riley, and Caden. Our two boys were diagnosed with a very rare liver disease in 2010, and now in 2014 have been confirmed healed, in Jesus' name. This true life story and testimony are about our battle for an answer, and for the faith to believe for it.

My prayer is that, as you read this book, you will expect miracles and breakthroughs in your own life. Our God is the God who heals, restores, and makes all things new. I pray that you will be touched by the hand of God, and that His Holy Spirit will fill you and rest upon you. (Numbers 11:24-25)

-- Korene Sturtz

MY GOD-STORY

This is the true story of a family in Clinton, Iowa, with five wonderful children. Two of their children were diagnosed with a very rare liver disease. They were able to overcome many obstacles because of their perseverance. But little did they know what was about to happen in their lives. The Lord was preparing them for a greater plan than they could have ever imagined. Their story will encourage you, and bring hope to face every circumstance in your future.

Our first two children were healthy, active girls who hit all of their milestones on time or beforehand. They were good eaters and always on a schedule. They were satisfied for hours on their feedings, and their growth was in line with the national average chart.

When I was expecting our first son, Cameron, everything was great. He was born at thirty-eight weeks, a little blue, but healthy—a happy, satisfied baby.

Cameron was about three months old when he began to demonstrate unusual behaviors. No longer satisfied with his three-hour eating schedule, he began to nurse every hour to hour and a half. I was constantly feeding him.

Around the time Cameron turned eight months old, he grew weaker and vomited multiple times a week. He was never satisfied, he was irritable, did not sleep well, and cried like he was in pain. He required multiple visits to the doctor and the emergency room.

The doctors would send us home, and assure me there was nothing wrong with him. Even though he was sick, he had accomplished every milestone. Cameron was above average on his motor skills: at eight months he was walking, and he could run at nine months. When he was two years old, he had learned to ride a bicycle (without training wheels). He was a 'go-getter'.

When I tried to wean him from nursing at age two, Cameron would cry. It wasn't a rebellious cry, but a cry of pain. (Most moms know when there's something wrong with their children. This is a gift of discernment the Lord gives.) Something was not quite right. A good eater but always hungry, he never seemed satisfied through the night. Around the age three, Cameron stopped nursing. He would wake up in the mornings very sick.

One morning Cameron was lightly crying in his bed. When I went into his room, he was lying there, his face pale in color with yellow undertones. Dark circles under his eyes that were gray in color, and he was so weak that he could not even lift his head. I picked him up and carried him downstairs to the couch. He had dry heaves for two hours, spitting up yellow bile. I tried to give him hot tea and toast, but he was unable to keep anything down.

I called the doctor and took him in to see her; she had no explanation for his symptoms, so we were sent home. Cameron was so weak and sick that it took him seven and a half hours to fully recover. He would not move from the couch unless I carried him, and he could not eat or drink without getting sick. He eventually fell asleep. When he awoke, he ate more than I had ever seen him eat.

This became the norm. These episodes would occur as infrequently as once a month to as many as five times a week, and would last up to eight hours before Cameron regained the ability to walk, or to eat without getting sick.

During this time I became pregnant with Riley, Cameron's younger sister. The pregnancy was perfect, and the baby nursed on schedule. She was a perfectly healthy baby girl. Now I monitored Cameron's health, took care of baby Riley, and homeschooled Cameron's older sister, Madison.

When he was four years old, Cameron woke up with intermittent abdominal pain so severe it caused him to scream and cry. He could not even walk.

We rushed Cameron to his pediatrician, and she immediately admitted him to the local hospital. He was in the hospital for two days with no relief from the extreme pain. The doctors could not find the problem, so they transported him to a bigger hospital.

Think about this for a moment: Your four-year-old child is screaming in pain for two days in the hospital, and no one can help you.

Cameron was seen by a gastroenterologist but, to my surprise, they found nothing, and we were sent home to handle this on our own. The pain was now a new addition to Cameron's episodes. We continued to pray and believe for answers.

I was determined to find answers. For the next two years, Cameron continued to experience severe abdominal pain along with the episodes described earlier. Even though this daily battle continued, I read books, watched documentaries, called hospitals, talked to the specialist, prayed, and persevered in the Word of God; I knew the Lord had the answer.

Cameron was admitted to the Iowa City Children's Hospital for tests. The specialist did blood work, brain scans, x-rays, and many other tests. She presented a possible diagnosis: abdominal migraines.

As soon as she said it, my motherly instinct kicked in. I knew in that moment it was the wrong diagnosis, and refused to give him the medication she prescribed. The doctors were not very understanding of my decision, so we left the hospital, and I drove home once again with no answers, pleading to the Lord for help.

Several weeks passed, and Cameron returned to his pediatrician. Exhausted, I continued looking for answers.

Cameron began to have severe headaches, so we went back to the children's hospital in Iowa City to see the neurology team.

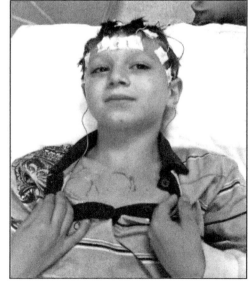

The tests took five days. The doctors told Cameron to stay in bed for those five days, hooked up to sixty different brain electrodes, and they ran a fasting test, where he was not allowed to eat or leave his room for twelve hours. Picture a very active five-year-old boy forced to sit still for five days. The doctors believed this would "throw" Cameron into an episode.

He was ill, but his blood sugar never dropped below seventy, so they were not concerned. Hindsight is 20/20. If they would have checked his blood ketones, they would have found a toxic amount in his blood. He was nauseous to the point of vomiting. At the end of these five days, the doctors determined that nothing was wrong.

Again, they had no conclusive answers. They suggested that we feed Cameron protein at bedtime to see if it would help. The doctors believed he had an over-active metabolism and was burning more energy than his body could absorb. They told me to make sure Cameron did not sleep in, to check his blood sugars, and to feed him as soon as he awoke in the morning.

This seemed to help minimize the episodes, but they never stayed away for long.

Within three weeks, we were back to where we started. Day after day, week after week, the same episodes continued. I wanted to give up, but knew in my heart there was an answer somewhere, so we continued to pray and ask the Lord to help Cameron. We had a supportive family and church, and many friends prayed for and came alongside us in our fight.

Had I done something to cause my son's pain and sickness?

As a child, I was sexually abused for years. This caused many illnesses for me, one of which was cervical cancer. I underwent treatment and surgery, and half of my cervix was removed. The surgery revealed scar tissue and endometriosis. The specialist explained that I would never be able to have children.

When I met my husband, he already had a daughter, Aubriana. I instantly accepted her as my daughter, and believed that I would not have any more children. A few years passed, and I found out that I was pregnant. I was in shock, and was told to be on light duty. We found out that he was a baby boy, and a week later we lost him. One year later, I became pregnant with our daughter, Madison. She was born a little early, but was perfectly healthy.

Then I became pregnant again within a year, and once again found out that it was a boy, but lost him within a week. I was devastated, but happy for the two girls I had.

Once again, I became pregnant, but before we knew what the baby was, I miscarried.

I remembered our three babies in heaven. I knew that two of them were boys. My mind was on overload.

During my pregnancy with Cameron, I took vitamins for energy, and thought that perhaps this caused his increased metabolism. I began to feel the guilt and condemnation come upon me. I was so sad for my son. I repented over and over again. I thought that condemnation was from the Lord, but that is not true. Conviction comes from the Lord, not condemnation. For years I believed I had caused this sickness that the doctors could not diagnose.

As Cameron grew, his health became worse. He was the happiest boy, loving and affectionate to everyone. His smile and joy filled every room he entered. However, when Cameron experienced an episode, he became easily irritated, and felt sick with bad headaches off and on throughout the day. He became too weak to walk without help.

Cameron was five and a half years old when his little brother, Caden, was born. For the first week Caden was the best baby boy. He was happy, healthy, and he nursed well. I noticed familiar symptoms when Caden had to fast before his circumcision. He was sick for two days, cranky, unsatisfied, easily irritated, and he wanted to nurse all the time. I tried to tell myself he was in pain from the surgery.

Caden's eating schedule changed continually. He was only happy when he was nursing. This was familiar. Cameron had been the same way when he was a baby, always wanting to nurse, and irritable when he wasn't eating. I allowed Caden to sleep with me every night and nursed him, it seemed, all night long. We got very little sleep. This continued for two years.

The doctors wanted me to start monitoring everything the boys ate and drank, and to write down the amount and the time of day, so I kept food logs for weeks.

We now had four children. I was homeschooling, and two of them had these episodes for years with no diagnosis or help from the medical world. I tried to research their health symptoms, but to no avail. I had many sleepless, worry-filled nights, not knowing what else to do but pray and trust God for an answer.

Now that we had another sick child, I was overwhelmed. I could no longer provide my children with the attention and the teaching they needed for school, so we put Madison, and Cameron into private school for a couple years, during which time we took Cameron and Caden to our local pediatrician several times a month. The pediatrician was doing all she could, but still had no diagnosis to offer.

In August 2009, when Caden was two years old, I had weaned him from nursing. Even though he no longer was breastfeeding, he still woke up twice per night to drink milk from a sippy cup.

I continued to give Cameron high protein at bedtime, and waking him by 7:00 a.m. to test his blood sugar.

The doctor suggested the 7:00 a.m. wake-up to prevent him from getting sick. If he slept past 7:00 a.m., he would be sick for up to seven hours. The doctor believed Cameron was simply overly active.

Even though I followed the doctor's suggestions, Cameron still woke up sick. I sought help from any specialist that would talk to me. Once again we suggested another appointment with another specialist; they scheduled another weeklong test. Even though years had passed, Cameron, now seven, still had many episodes. The tests were always prolonged, and invasive to the point that I had a hard time sleeping because Cameron would cry out in pain.

I would lie in the hospital bed, holding him and praying, "Lord, please help us."

Tests once again revealed no diagnosis. The doctors would see some of the symptoms, but never to the extent we experienced them at home. We wondered why no one could help us.

I was scared. This disease was truly wearing on him. Many friends and family members also began to see it slowly suck the life out of Cameron. They would ask, "Why is Cameron so gray? What is wrong with him?"

During Christmas break in 2009, Caden slowly came downstairs, and said he felt very sick. He was pale with yellow undertones. There were dark circles under his eyes. He was sweating and shaking. My stomach sank.

I made hot tea and cinnamon toast for him, and held him. Four or five hours passed before he felt well enough to get off the couch.

I talked to Darin about Caden's episode, and asked him what he thought. He thought it might just be the flu. I didn't think about it anymore, until five days later when it happened again. This time it was worse.

My heart sank. I thought, *"What have I done? What could be wrong with my boys?"* and cried, "Lord, please help me. Lord, help me."

I had told Darin that if Caden had another episode we would need to take him to the hospital.

By this time, we had a glucometer for Cameron to test his blood sugar on the mornings when he was sick to see if he had a slight form of hypoglycemia. Cameron was now eight, and Caden was two years and three months old. He still slept with us because he would cry for milk in the night.

One evening in January 2010, we had an unforgettable experience. This incident will be planted in my brain forever as a reminder of how far we have come. Caden was sleeping between Darin and me in our bed. Around 2:00 a.m., I heard Caden softly whining. As I reached over and touched him, he was sweaty, but clammy; and his little heart was beating so hard I felt it through the blanket.

I scooped Caden's weak little body up in my arms and woke Darin. We carried Caden downstairs. I grabbed Cameron's glucometer and tested Caden's blood sugar level. It was a thirty-two.

Terrified, I called 911 while Darin held Caden as he lost consciousness. I was so nervous, I accidentally hung up. Then I called the doctor, but there was no answer. I was shaking.

Our other three children heard the commotion, climbed out of bed, and sat frightened at the top of the stairs as they watched this unfold.

I called 911 again, and as I talked to the dispatcher on the phone, I was able to drip a little fruit juice under Caden's tongue, desperately attempting to get his blood sugar up. He was unconscious for fifteen to twenty minutes before the ambulance arrived. He was rushed to our local hospital, and then transported to Iowa City Children's Hospital.

I held Caden in the ambulance as the EMTs tried to get an IV started. They were unsuccessful.

I was determined not to leave the hospital until I had an answer that could help my boys.

That morning in Iowa City, as the doctors assessed Caden's condition, I suggested that we see a pediatric geneticists' team. The doctors agreed with me, and the geneticists' team came in and went through our family's medical history.

This may sound confusing to some people, but I was excited to hear that this could be a genetic disease. If we could figure out what was wrong with one of the boys, we would know what was wrong with the other.

Once again, they had to undergo a series of painful tests. I had to hold them as the doctors did skin biopsies.

Skin biopsies were taken using hole-punches through all the layers of the skin on their upper arms without painkillers. It was torturous. We were told that it could take a few months to get the test results back, but the doctor felt confident that the boys had a rare genetic disease called *Glycogen Storage Disease IX*. At the time, less than one hundred people in the world were diagnosed with GSD IX. We would treat the boys' symptoms with a small amount of Argo Corn Starch at bedtime, which should help keep them stable, but they would not be able to fast for any reason. The specialist explained that the boys were getting sick because their blood sugar kept dropping.

I was able to get a little relief because now I had an answer. My boys would be fine.

We were sent home with the cornstarch diet. You can guess what happened. It worked for two weeks, and then the boys began to have more episodes with bad headaches, muscle cramps, and weakness.

I continued to call the medical geneticist, and he tried to help by increasing the cornstarch levels for both boys. Every night I would wake up and mix the cornstarch with milk, wake the boys at midnight, and they would drink their dose. We did this every night.

Even though I gave them protein at bedtime, cornstarch throughout the day and night, and awoke them in the morning to feed them, they were still sickly.

Once again, I took them back to the pediatrician and requested to go to another hospital for a second opinion. We were given an appointment at Mayo Clinic, but had to wait a few months to see the doctor there. The episodes grew worse. This went on from March 2010, when we were last at the Iowa City Hospital, until October, when we were scheduled to go to the Mayo Clinic.

I was frustrated once again. I cried, "Lord, help me! Help me figure out what is wrong." I could not stand to see my boys so sick all the time.

Cameron was now nine years old, and Caden was three. While all of this was happening, I still maintained our home, helped my husband run our business, and took care of five children. Since I could not help Darin very much, he had to do other things to support us, so he wasn't able to help much with the children. Our extended family wanted to help, but they were scared because of the worsened condition of the boys. Our children stayed with me.

My mom graciously helped me take the boys to their appointments at Mayo Clinic, while the girls stayed with

Darin. There were several appointments set up, and once again a lot of lab work, and more painful medical tests for the boys to endure. We spent three months, weeks at a time, going from one appointment to another, one specialist to another. I almost gave up because of all the invasive tests that my boys had to endure without painkillers. (Note: The chemicals in the painkillers would have interfered with the test results.)

One test required Caden to fast from midnight to 7:00 a.m. I had explained to the doctor that, because Caden's blood sugars dropped, I had been told he should not fast for any reason, and he had to take cornstarch in the night. The doctor reassured me he would be fine, to give him his 8:00 p.m. cornstarch, skip his midnight feeding, and bring him to the first appointment the next morning.

I did as she requested, and by the time we made it to Caden's morning appointment, he was unconscious. His blood sugar level was forty-two. The doctor ignored me and disregarded Caden's symptoms. I assumed she didn't have any idea what this was. After all the tests were completed, we left the hospital, not feeling that the doctor had listened to us.

A couple weeks after the boys' last appointment, the doctor called and asked us to come see her for the results. We sat in the office, anticipating good news. The doctor told us the boys had *Glycogen Storage Disease IX Alpha-2*. She explained that this was good because it is a benign disease, which meant that there are no symptoms and no problems, and no known health effects to the body.

I asked, "Then, Doctor, why do they have all of these symptoms?"

To my shock, she proceeded to ask what I might be doing to cause their symptoms. She assumed that I was either making up their symptoms, or causing them.

Her accusations caused me to doubt what I was actually seeing. I thought maybe there was something in our home causing their illness, but then why would no one else in our family be sick?

I was discouraged, but my faith in the Lord never wavered.

I wept and prayed every day for answers. I knew I had to be strong and have faith for not just myself but for my children. Children are a gift from the Lord, and that there was a purpose, a reason, for this. I prayed, believing that answers would come soon.

It was around this time that the Lord sent two people to me. One was from our community, and the other from our church. They both said that the Lord had impressed upon them to share a story with me. They reminded me about the story Jesus told of the persistent widow who kept going to the judge's door to beg for help day after day, even in the evening, until she got her answer. She never gave up.

"Then Jesus told his disciples a parable to show them that they should always pray and not give up. ² He said: "In a certain town there was a judge who neither feared God nor cared what people thought. ³ And there was a widow in that town who kept coming to him with the plea, 'Grant me justice against my adversary.' ⁴ "For some time he refused. But finally he said to himself, 'Even though I don't fear God or care what people think, ⁵ yet because this widow keeps bothering me, I will see that she gets justice, so that she won't eventually come and attack me!'" ⁶ And the Lord said, "Listen to what the unjust judge says. ⁷ And will not God bring about justice for

his chosen ones, who cry out to him day and night?
Will he keep putting them off? ⁸ I tell you, he will see
that they get justice, and quickly. However, when the
Son of Man comes, will he find faith on the earth?"
(Luke 18:1-8, NIV)

"To persist in prayer and not give up does not mean endless repetition nor painfully long prayer sessions. Always praying means keeping our request constantly before God as we live for Him each day, believing He will answer. When we live by faith, we are not to give up. God may delay answering, but His delays always have good reasons. As we persist in prayer we grow in character, faith, and hope. In this story we need to know that if an unjust judge responds to constant pressure, how much more will a great and loving God respond to us. If we know He loves us, we can believe He will hear our cries for help."(*Life Application Study Bible, New International Version*)

This passage encouraged me, and I held on to every word received from the Lord. I was convinced help was out there. I once again evaluated everything that I was doing, and everything the boys were doing and eating.

By this time it was early 2011, and their episodes had worsened. I contacted the pediatric geneticist in Iowa City Children's Hospital on a weekly basis until he realized I was not going to give up. Eventually he admitted that he could not help us. I was impressed by the doctor's humility in referring us to another specialist who only dealt with *Glycogen Storage*

Disease (GSD). This time I did not get overly excited. I was willing to do anything or see anyone to help my children.

The new specialist was located in Gainesville, Florida, at the University of Florida's *Glycogen Storage Disease Research Clinic*. We explained to the new doctor our years of testing, all of the episodes, and our multiple trips to the emergency room each month. But our story did not scare this doctor away. He said it sounded like he could help us. Now it was time to pray even more, and to wait upon the Lord.

This is where it gets good. I realized the only hope I had was in the Lord. He had given me strength to persevere and to keep fighting for answers. I knew He was in charge. During the months of waiting, the Lord told me I would one day write a book. I knew it was God, because I had never had the desire to write.

In May 2011, He gave me what I thought would be the title of my book—"A Mother's Plea"—referring to my prayers and petitions. The purpose of the book would be to encourage others to persevere until they get their answers. It was to let everyone know that the only way is through the Father's grace, and by His strength alone. The Lord was going to use our story to help others understand that, no matter how small or big the trials they face, He alone is the answer.

This trip to Florida would be a pivotal point in our story. We all packed up and flew to Florida as a family to see what we might do to help our boys.

This is three-year-old Caden after he got settled into his bed. His IV was hurting him, but he was brave.

The nurses and doctors were wonderful, and cared for the boys. They brought them gifts, and a video game to play on the television.I slept in Caden's bed and Cameron was next to us in his bed. Every hour on the hour, for four days, blood was drawn. It was a difficult week.

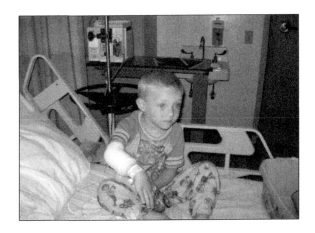

Our family made it as fun as possible. The kids joined in and stayed at the hospital. They played games with the boys and went on scavenger hunts for little lizards. This picture shows how close we were as a family.

Our first visit with the specialist in Florida was on June 11, 2011.

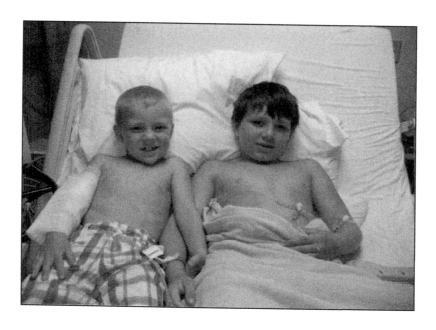

This will give you an idea of the things the boys had to go through to get an answer:

1. They shared a room
2. They were hooked up to blood pressure monitors, oxygen monitors and IV's for five days.
3. Every hour on the hour, for the first four days, blood had to be drawn.
4. Their IV's had to be changed multiple times due to their veins collapsing from all the blood draws.
5. One of those days, two of Caden's veins were blown out, which was very painful.

By the end of the five days we had a clearer understanding of the disease, and the aggressive treatments that would be required to stabilize the boys. We finally had answers. Excitement filled the room, because the doctors said that with this treatment the boys would be able to live normal lives.

Glycogen Storage Disease Type IX Alpha-2 was their diagnosis. *Glycogen Storage Diseases* (GSDs) are inherited genetic disorders on the X chromosome that cause glycogen to be improperly formed or released in the body. This results in a buildup of abnormal amounts, or types of glycogen in tissues.

Type IX is a liver glycogen phosphorylase kinase (enzyme) deficiency. Glycogen is mainly stored in the liver or in muscle tissue, so GSDs usually affect liver or muscle function, or both. The buildup of glycogen also prevents the body from keeping normal glucose levels, which causes a toxic amount of ketones to be released into the blood stream, causing these terrible episodes.

We were told that as long as we managed the boys' eating and cornstarch feedings, they would be fine. But if their sugars and blood ketones grew unstable, it could cause unconsciousness, seizures, and even death.

This information helped me understand why the boys nursed all the time in the night. Because I nursed them as often as I did, it saved their lives. Many babies with this aggressive disease, lose their lives in the night because their bodies starve to death.

To prevent the low blood sugars and high ketone levels, our boys had to be put on an aggressive eating schedule and treatment. The treatment was very detailed. For Cameron, we had to test his blood four times a day with a glucometer and a ketone-meter. The doctor put Cameron on 90 grams of cornstarch a day, split into three different feedings throughout the day and one at midnight.

For Caden, we had to test his blood four times a day, including one time in the middle of the night. The doctor also put Caden on 90 grams of cornstarch, which was split into four feedings per day.

Cameron's last feeding was at 9:00 p.m., we woke him at midnight for a feeding, and he had to be awakened by 6:00 a.m. for testing.

Caden's feeding schedule was a little more time-consuming. His last feeding was at 8:00 p.m., but I had to get up at midnight to do blood tests and another feeding. Caden also had to be up by 6:00 a.m. for blood tests.

Below is a picture of the supplies we needed daily:

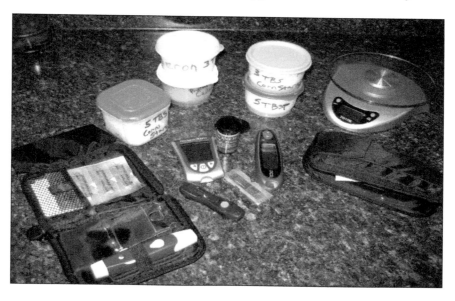

We returned home, and I was excited and thankful to finally have an answer. I talked with friends and family, and explained that something more needed to be done to raise people's awareness of this rare, mysterious disease, so we held a benefit fundraiser for *Glycogen Storage Disease Type IX*.

I talked with the team of doctors in Florida, set a time in October of 2011. Dr. David Weinstein, our guest speaker, explained the disease and latest research. He told us about the funds needed to continue the research. The benefit was a huge success. We had many volunteers who helped, and our community stood with us.

More than six hundred wonderful people attended, and gave over $35,000 to help pay our medical expenses. Plus, we were able to donate over $20,000 to the GSD research program at the University of Florida in Gainesville.

The prescribed treatment that we were sent home to do only worked for about three months. Then the boys began to get sick more often.

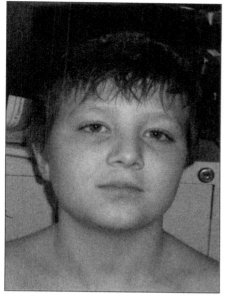

This is a picture of Cameron, who would get so weak that it was hard for him to stand up. The skin under his eyes would start to turn gray.

I documented our experiences, took pictures, and emailed them to the doctor, waiting for answers. I began to lose hope and faith in what the doctor had told us.

In October 2011, before the benefit, during a time with the Father, He reminded me of the book I was to write. I tried to make excuses. However, as you know, Father God does not listen to excuses. He said, "Daughter, I will help you write your story. It will give hope to the hopeless."

I broke down weeping. I recognized in that moment what the Lord was telling me: He would not take my boys with this disease. He would heal them!

During this year of adjustment with the diagnosis, many things began to unfold. The boys continued to get sick. Each week, we talked with the doctors in Florida, then with the doctor in Iowa City, and with their local pediatrician. We scheduled a yearly visit to the specialist in Florida, a visit every three months to the Iowa City specialist, and a monthly visit to the pediatrician.

We learned to work together with these three teams of wonderful doctors. They soon realized I was not going to give up, nor was I going to stop looking for answers.

One day, the local *Make-A-Wish* volunteers contacted us. The doctor in Iowa City had written to them about us. Our boys were *Make-A-Wish* kids in 2012. Cameron wanted to go on the Disney Cruise, but because of our concern with his health, we compromised. It would be Disney World instead.

That was a great family trip, and lots of memories were made, but travel was hard on the boys. Remember, even though it was fun, the feedings had to go on as scheduled. We had to continue the special diets and the blood value checks, and Caden was sick from the time we left home until two days after we arrived in Florida.

Caden's wish was to have a new playground. As a family, we wanted the best for our boys, yet we knew what this would mean: losing the garage in the middle of our backyard. Family and neighbors came over to help tear it down and prepare the ground for Caden's gift. The entire process was one long celebration.

God continually showed us how much He loves us, even in the midst of our trials. He even uses playgrounds for His glory..

Glycogen Storage Disease Type IX had only been seriously researched for five to seven years before we received the diagnosis. The doctor in Florida was doing as much as he could, with the few resources available to him. He was always available when we called him. He guided us and talked to the emergency room doctors in our area every time we had to take the boys to the ER. There was not a lot of information available about the disease, and the information online never commented on extreme cases like ours. We were told that our boys were the most severe case they had seen, and that they had multiple genetic mutations that had not been seen before. The specialist had told us that, with this type of disease, there would be no chance of a liver transplant because the disease is also in the skeletal muscles.

Soon after our first visit to Florida, Caden woke up lethargic and unable to move. We went to the emergency room, where we had to wait in the waiting room until they were ready for us. I was angry because Caden could not even lift his head. We learned very quickly to be pro-active. After that incident, the specialist in Florida prepared an emergency protocol sheet for us. We met with the hospital and emergency room directors, and explained to them why our boys needed immediate attention when we come into the ER. They were quite receptive. They made copies of this protocol sheet, and I met with their staff to explain my boys' condition. We were well known in the ER as the Sturtz boys' family.

The more I researched about the GSD, the more I met with doctors and teachers. The local pediatrician began to rely on my documentation. I also gained a lot of respect in the ER department of our local hospital. The doctors understood we were not there to mess around or to exaggerate the symptoms. We were there to get help when needed. We would only take the boys to the ER if the boys could not be stabilized at home. We would also call the Florida specialist for medical direction before going to the ER. He taught me how to read lab work, which labs were important, what the boys' lab values should be, and when to be concerned.

The boys continued to be sick on a weekly basis. One day, mid-morning, Caden was playing. It was usually a good time of day for him. Suddenly, he lay down on the floor and told me he was dying. He said his chest was hurting badly, and that he needed to go to the hospital. He kept crying that he was dying. I asked him if he felt sick, shaky, or weak. He said, "I'm just dying."

We rushed him to the ER to find out that his cardiac enzymes were three times higher than it should be, and his liver enzymes were also elevated. This would continue for days, weeks, months, and years. Cameron would also get sick, but his was always headache-related, and his muscles would become so weak he couldn't walk. His lab work, also abnormal, revealed damage to his liver and skeletal muscles.

The year of 2012 was tough. We had new feedings to contend with, more doctor visits, and little new information. We returned to Florida for more tests. The doctor had found more people with this disease, but not the same mutations as our boys. He did not understand why we were having so much trouble, and began to wonder what else he could do to help.

Here are some pictures of the boys during this visit.

The daily schedule in our home never seemed to slow down. Since 2010, our boys dietary restrictions consisted of little to no sugar at all, as little fat as possible, and high protein.

Cameron was now eleven years old. His liver was enlarged. He had muscle weakness and pain on a daily basis, and was sometimes unable to walk.

The boys had to be in bed between 8:00 and 9:00 p.m., get up early every morning, then test their blood glucose and ketones to determine the amount of cornstarch for that morning dose. They would eat a high-protein breakfast followed by their first dose of corn starch. They would then have a snack consisting of 5-10 grams of protein, eat lunch, then test their blood values one hour after eating and take another dose of cornstarch. They would eat an afternoon high-protein snack, test their blood before dinner, eat dinner, and have a snack an hour before bedtime. Then around 8:00 to 9:00 p.m., they would take another dose of cornstarch.

At midnight they would take another dose of cornstarch, and wake in the morning to start all over again. Cameron started needing 90 grams of cornstarch and 90 grams of protein daily. Caden started needing 90 grams of cornstarch and 45 grams of protein daily. By the end of 2012, Cameron was taking 165 grams of cornstarch and 135 grams of protein, and having four blood value checks a day. Caden was taking 135 grams of cornstarch, one feeding at midnight, and another at 3:00 a.m., with blood checks before each feeding. He required 80 grams of protein, and four to five blood value checks a day.

I kept blood value logs, food logs, measured cornstarch, and tried to monitor everything the boys put into their mouths. Every three hours, around the clock, I made sure their blood values were stable.

The Lord's grace was upon my life the entire time. One cannot raise five children, help with the family business, take care of the medical needs of two special needs children, sleep four to six hours a night, two hours at a time, maintain a house, and serve at the church without the grace, mercy, forgiveness, strength, love, and peace of Father God.

In the fall of 2012, our community helped us with another fundraiser. It was trivia night. We raised around $5,000 to help with the increasing medical bills and travel expenses for the boys.

On January 27, 2013, the Lord reminded me that the purpose of this book was to connect with others who battle rare diseases. With a mother's heart, and by acting upon His Word, I am to show compassion and the love of Christ to others who are going through similar challenges on a daily basis.

Many things happened in 2013. At the beginning of the year, everything seemed to be going in the same direction—downhill. Cameron began to struggle in school. He had difficulty with his short-term memory, and with his vision. He could not sit still and listen to his teachers. He did not understand the homework instructions. Every evening, including weekends, we would help him with homework for three to five hours, basically re-teaching everything he had learned that day.

We decided to take him to a specialist in Iowa City Children's Hospital. That meant we had several appointments again. The specialists performed all the tests that were available.

I had done my own research on the lack of glucose to the brain in young children, and the long-term effects and damage this may cause to the neurotransmitters in the brain. I submitted my research to the specialist in Florida for review. He said it could be a possibility, not only because of all of the years Cameron went without a diagnosis, but because, along with the toxic amounts of blood ketones, his glucose levels were averaging in the very low range below normal.

I began to wonder what other side effects of this disease might have taken hold of him before the diagnosis. The specialist said he did not have ADHD or ADD, but he definitely had many deficiencies. Once again, no one could give us an answer. We would meet with Cameron's teachers each week, but they were starting to run short on understanding and patience. Darin and I decided to meet with all the local district school staff and administrators to see what they could do to help us.

As we met several times with the public school leaders, I sat in the meetings weeping. It seemed as if no one understood what I was saying. Yes, they wanted to help, but they had no idea to what extent this disease affected everything.

My brain was on overload. I prayed again for direction. Once again, we sought the Lord for a breakthrough for our family.

Caden continued to come to me at least three days a week, lie on the floor, and tell me he was dying. He would be very persistent and straightforward. I assured he would be fine, and would test his blood. Most of the time, the values were normal. He insisted that the meters were wrong. Some days this would go on for hours. I would take a picture, email it to the doctor, and ask what to do next. We would again go get the twelve labs drawn, and they would show more liver damage, more skeletal muscle damage, but the liver and cardiac values would be abnormal.

Would this ever end?

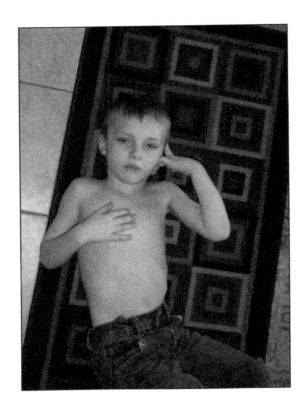

On March 2013, we attended a friend's church to hear a guest speaker. Though I was feeling a lot of pain in my upper abdomen, I decided to go, expecting something great. Darin was out of town, I thought, but he surprised me by walking in as the service began.

The speaker, Ed Trout, is a gifted prophet (one who hears from and speaks for God). At one point during the service, he suddenly looked at us and spoke words of encouragement. It was as if Father God was standing in front of us, speaking directly to us. The word, directed toward Darin, was this:

"A wonderful quality God's wanting from you is that you will do stuff, but you don't feel like

you're always so spiritual. You don't want to push yourself forward, because you think that is not who you are. But that is who you are, because you are real. You are 'Integris.' You are the real deal. People love you. People can come to you, can tell you all kinds of stuff, and you don't repeat it or judge them. God loves you for that.

You have been done wrong… There have been injustices done more than once. But the Lord says, 'I am your Dad, and I am going to do you well. I am going to lift you up and give you inheritances. I will take care of you. I bless you, but I am knocking on your door. I need to use you, because people want to follow you. You are a natural leader, people love you, and it's that simple.'"

This gentleman had never met us or talked with us before. The Lord gave him these words to speak, and we knew they were from the Lord. This man then looked at me and said:

"You are a dreamer, but you've stopped trying to understand God speaking to you in dreams. It's too strange, too weird. God says you need to wake that up again because He wants to speak prophetically through you and to you.

There is a sister or someone who has become estranged, and a strain in the relationship. God's going to heal that by His spirit. Nothing is too hard for the Lord.

As He is speaking to me now, He says that He is healing you of something, some pain, and when

*you leave, the pain will be gone. Every symptom will
be gone, because God is a healer. He is The Healer.*

*You have five children, and one has a
struggle. You have done everything for him. It's not
because of anything you have done wrong, but it's a
struggle. God says He's going to take care of it. In
fact, he is going to become a blessing, just be patient.*

*God says, 'I use these things for a purpose.
Trust Me. I will do something great with this,
okay?'"*

We left encouraged that evening. By the time we left,
the pain and swelling in my abdomen were gone. I knew that
the Lord was our Healer, and I praised Him for that.

This began a new awakening in me. I began to have
dreams—and not only to have dreams, but to understand
what the Lord was saying to me. (I was able to interpret those
dreams.)

On April 30, 2013, Darin had a dream. Afterwards, we
read these verses:

- Ephesians 5:26,
- Genesis 49:4,
- Proverbs 18:4,
- John 4:14,
- John 7:38;
- Isaiah 9:6,
- Ezekiel 16:44,
- Luke 15:13, and
- 1 Corinthians 28:20.

As we pondered this idea, prayed and dug into the
Bible, we believed the Lord was showing us that we needed
to put to death everything that was out of order in our

spiritual and business lives. Darin was walking in the Spirit of the Lord. The Lord wanted him to worship, to function in the gifts of the Spirit, and to flow in the gift of service (Isaiah 41:18). When Darin positioned himself under the structure of God's authority and committed to the full covenant with Christ, there would be victory over the enemy and Darin would receive His anointing (Psalms 23:5).

On May 6, 2013, I had a dream. This was the second dream that month in which I was pregnant. Pregnancy is a sign of new life, a new birth, waiting, appropriation in process, expectation (Matthew 20:22). When you are pregnant with an idea that the Lord puts on your heart, walk through it. When it's time, He will deliver it.

In the beginning, no one can see that you are pregnant. But once you start moving toward the delivery date, they *can* see it. Make it all the way to the delivery. Don't abort this idea. Don't experience a miscarriage. Wait for God's timing.

For the previous two weeks I had been waking up singing worship songs. I want to worship God, I want to prophesy, I have a deep desire to be closer to him, and I am fully devoted.

On June 30, 2013, the Lord told me to read Matthew chapters 9 and 10. Chapter 10 talks about Jesus sending out the twelve disciples. Jesus gave the disciples a principle to guide their actions as they ministered to others: *"Freely you have received, freely give."*

Because God has showered us with His blessings, we should give generously of our time, our love, and our possessions. Jesus said that those who minister are to be cared for. The disciples could expect food and shelter in return for the spiritual service they provided. Who ministers to you? Make sure you help care for the pastors, missionaries, and teachers who serve God by serving you.

Mark's account says to take a staff, but Matthew and Luke say not to. Jesus may have meant that they were not to take an *extra* staff, bag, or a pair of sandals. In any case, the principle was that they were prepared, unencumbered by excess material goods, ready for duty and for travel. So we are supposed to take care of the people who minister to us, and to be prepared at all times to minister to others.

On July 28, 2013, I was driving to church, and the Lord reminded me of the story of Abraham and Isaac. During my quiet time that morning, the Lord told me that we are overcomers, because He overcame. The story of Abraham and Isaac was my reminder.

When the Lord told Abraham to get his son Isaac and prepare him as a sacrifice, Abraham did not grumble or complain. He did not fear the Lord's request; he trusted, had faith, and he obeyed the Lord without reservation. Abraham did not fret; he believed that the Lord had a great and mighty plan. As I pondered that story, the Lord showed me how we are to deal with our circumstances, how we are to respond to life's pressures. It is what determines the glory He receives. We are to have faith, to trust, and to obey Him.

I was on stage with the worship team when the Lord told me to write that down and share it with Pastor Steve. As I worshiped in song, in my spirit, I was arguing with the Lord. I was concerned with what people would think as I was looking for a pen, trying to be obedient but still worshiping.

The Lord reminded me of the phrase, *"Whom shall I fear?"* Do I fear man or Him?

I told Him I would obey.

The Lord told me there was a pen on the floor behind me. I turned, grabbed it, and wrote down the words He told me to say. It was a message for our church:

We need to praise the Lord through our circumstances, have faith, and trust Him always. Because of our obedience, the Lord will bless us. Now or later, it does not matter, because He knows what is best for us. Remember, how we deal with our circumstances and the situations of life will determine the level of His glory on us in the end.

On August 11, 2013, I had a dream in which the Lord said, "Get your house in order." This dream was to encourage me to keep moving forward with Him, but to repent always, and not to lose sight of the sins that always try to creep up on me. I was to keep them under my feet, and to remain submitted to Christ.

We have the power to defeat the enemy. In Romans 16:20, we are told that Satan is under our feet because of the grace of our Lord Jesus. So it is time to get our houses in alignment with the Father's plans and desires, not forgetting the enemy also has a plan for us. We are to be strong and believe that things will get better. This was especially difficult for me, because during this time our boys were still sickly and in decreasing health.

I had another dream in August 2013. In this dream it seemed I was being led by a manipulating spirit. The Lord was asking me to consider my motives for my boys' healing. Was my motive to save myself the pain and embarrassment, or was it to bring God glory and honor? The Lord was showing me that no matter what obstacles and problems I may have to go through, and sometimes *choose* to go through, He is always there for me and waiting for me to make the correct decision.

With the dreams, the Lord was preparing me for the next phase in my life.

Our next trip to Florida to see the specialist was scheduled for the last week of August 2013.

We got the boys situated in the hospital, and the doctor had to call a special team in to set the IVs, which took over two hours for each boy.

Cameron's liver had increased up to five times the normal size, and now his spleen was compromised. His spleen was twice the normal size, and was attempting to make up for what the liver could not do. Cameron was getting weaker and having more headaches. He was becoming more confused, it was harder for him to understand things, and he had difficulty expressing himself. He could not tell a story in chronological order. It was quite confusing for me and frustrating for him.

Caden was malnourished, unable to hold food down, and refusing to eat because he always felt sick. He wanted to eat cornstarch instead of food. Every time we attempted to get

Caden to eat anything, he would take one bite then refuse to eat. Or he would gag at the thought of eating.

As a family, we decided to do something different this time. Our first day in Florida, we read the Word and prayed together as a family. This practice was the turning point in our relationships with one another and with Christ, and continues to this day.

By the end of the boys' hospital stay, the doctor had talked to us about the condition of both boys. Their livers no longer stored iron. Their arteries were hardening, which caused their livers and spleens to enlarge. Cameron's liver was so compromised that it was almost to the point of *cirrhosis* (when healthy liver tissue is destroyed, and replaced by scar tissue; the condition becomes serious, as it can block the flow of blood through the liver). He would not be eligible for a transplant, because his skeletal muscles were breaking down. We would have to keep a close watch on him.

Malnourished, Caden was losing weight and having chest and muscle pain regularly. In the night, along with giving the boys their middle-of-the-night feedings, I would have to rub his legs and arms because of the muscle pain,.

During this stay, the doctor had us try a new night treatment. Cameron said it tasted like "dirty sock water." We all laughed, but he had to drink it. What a strong twelve year old. Now that Cameron could take this one feeding at bedtime, he could be stable all night. That gave me a break, and allowed him a full night's sleep. Now that was exciting!

Caden, on the other hand, could not even keep food down, let alone the nasty-tasting stuff. The doctor and the nurses did everything to get Caden to eat, or at least to drink protein to help him gain weight, but nothing helped. The doctor said if Caden did not eat, he wouldn't survive much longer. I was devastated.

I asked the doctor about a feeding tube for Caden. He said to give it another month, and we would see how he was doing.

We went home. Cameron was starting to look like he wanted to give up. Caden was sick daily because of the refusal to eat. And me? I was exhausted.

On September 13th, 2013, I attended a Joyce Meyer conference. During the evening worship time, the Lord gave me a vision. He came to my front door to take me on a walk. As we strolled down a path through a wooded area, He pointed at things along the path, all the things I had experienced in my life—all of the pain, the trials, and the lack of reassurance. He told me He had been with me through it all. He took me through my life story to show He was the one who rescued me from my past hurts, pains, and abuse.

As we drew closer to the most recent times of my life, we were nearing the edge of the woods. The Lord walked out of the wooded area, reached for my hand, and said, "Daughter, you have been in the wilderness long enough. It is time to walk into the promises I have for you."

With that, I crossed from the edge of the woods into the Promised Land with the Lord that day.

For those who do not know me, on November 6, 2013, I turned forty years of age. Moses and the Israelites were in the wilderness for forty years. It was my time. The Lord had planned something very special for me. I was able to tell others who said I was "over the hill" that I was now walking in the Father's promises, so watch out—something big was about to happen!

On September 29, 2013, the Lord led me to read Ruth, chapter 4. The Book of Ruth reports events that were part of God's preparations for the births of David and of Jesus, the promised Messiah.

> "As Ruth was unaware of this larger purpose in her life, we will not know the full purpose and importance of our lives until we are able to look back from the perspective of eternity. We must make our choices with God's eternal values in mind. Taking moral shortcuts and living for short range pleasures are not good ways to move ahead. Because of Ruth's faithful obedience, her life and legacy were significant even though she couldn't see all the results. Live in faithfulness to God, knowing that the significance of your life will extend beyond your lifetime. The rewards will outweigh any sacrifice you may have made."
>
> (From the footnotes in the NIV version regarding Ruth 4:16-17)

Darin and I often discussed the boys' health. He asked once if I was willing to give the boys to God. If the Lord's plan was to take them into heaven, would I be all right with that? I grew quite angry that he would even ask that. I was not ready to give up. I had fought for so long that I felt they would die if I gave up.

There must be an answer somewhere. The medical staff reminded me there was no medical cure. All we could hope for was to keep the boys stable.

I was scared. Although I was willing to receive their healing, I was not willing to yield their lives to the Lord. You see, my children were my life. I could not live my life without them. For many years, I even feared asking the Lord to heal them for fear that He would take them to heaven rather than heal them on earth.

I finally sincerely asked the Lord to heal my boys, not knowing what was about to happen. The next dream marked a milestone in my pursuit after God.

On October 14, 2013, I dreamed that I went into a shop and stood at the counter, where I had ordered flowers for myself, something I have never done. As I waited for the lady to get my order, I looked down at the left side of the counter on the floor, and saw a beautiful lavender plant. The lavender is known as spikenard in the Bible, and is used for healing and rest—both of which I greatly needed.

A sales lady then appeared with a vase of roses wrapped in yellow craft paper, and said I owed her $600. I was in shock. I asked her why $600. She said, "You ordered nine roses." I told her I did not order nine roses. She said nothing more.

But as I stood at the counter, I pondered buying the lavender plant, which less expensive than the nine roses.

Then I awoke.

Here was my interpretation:

- To my carnal mind, it would have been foolish to order nine roses for $600, but the Lord was showing me to have faith and to trust Him.
- The yellow craft paper around the roses represented a gift from God, *light* and *life*.
- Why the amount of $600? Six represents the number of man, flesh or carnality.

- Hundred represents fullness, or a full measure. So was I willing to pay the fullness of my carnality (or flesh) for this gift from God?
- The Lord told me the roses represent the nine gifts of the Spirit. (1 Corinthians 12:1-11)

For thirteen years, I had helped lead worship. Now the Lord told me to explore the Word of God and to see what other gifts He had for me. This was a difficult decision, but after many days of prayer, I obeyed the Father and I stepped down from the worship team.

By this time, the doctors were very concerned about Caden's health. We were in and out of the ER weekly. He wasn't eating, he was missing school, he was miserable, and he had lost a lot of weight and muscle mass. I encouraged the doctors to go ahead with the feeding tube surgery, relieved to think we were now on the same page. We set the appointment, and I thought this was going to be great. Caden was going to feel better, and I was going to get to rest and spend time with my *entire* family.

Caden's surgery was in October 2013 at University of Iowa Children's Hospital. He was a very sick boy. He had two IVs, four veins blown in three days. The flight paramedics had to administer the IVs, and they still had to poke him six times with a special machine to see the deep veins, because Caden's little veins would not allow them to thread the IV. He was brave; it took an hour and a half to get all the IVs set. They had to be changed three times in three days, and each time was worse than the last.

As I held my baby, weeping with him, the Lord said, "Can you imagine what My mother felt as she watched Me being beaten and crucified?"

At that moment, I knew it was going to be okay. My pain of watching my child endure this was not comparable to the pain Mary felt watching Jesus beaten and nailed to a cross. I could get through this, and so would Caden.

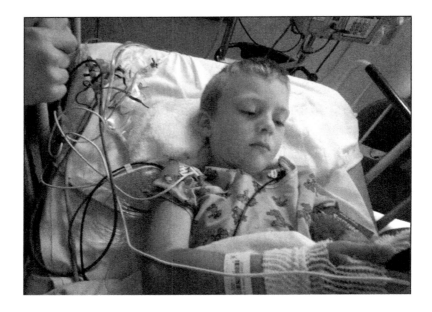

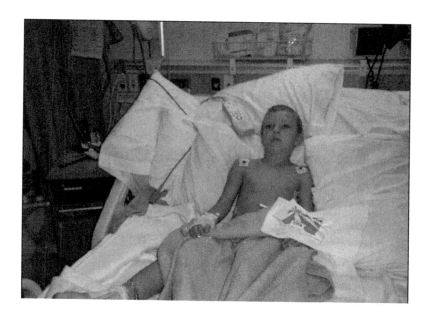

While we were in the hospital, I had another dream. It revealed many things that were going on in our lives. I will share some of the details, and leave others out, because some of the intimate details from the Lord were for me alone.

In that dream I had a baby boy, and he also had GSD, the same disease the other boys had. I was in a school, then, somewhat like a nursery, with nurses all around. Cameron was helping care for the baby. We had to take the sleeping baby to the back of my truck to change his diaper, and to return to the building we had to go through a very small yellow back door. I remember thinking in my dream that my breast milk was enough to keep him stable.

Suddenly we were somewhere else, and the skin on the top of the baby's head (his scalp) was split into two pieces. I was taking him to go get stitches, then we were at a friend's house, and I awoke.

Here was my interpretation:

- The baby represented a new beginning, desiring pure spiritual food.
- My son, the new baby boy, represented the unique (rare) ministry, and spiritual reproduction. This baby had the rare disease that my other two boys had…
- … Yet the baby was sleeping, and that represented rest, rejuvenation, blessing, and safety.
- The yellow door represented the entrance or a beginning, a new opportunity, a transition, a challenge for us to follow and endure.
- The color yellow represented a gift from or of God, light in life, family, honor.
- The school/hospital represented God's appropriation, healing, and restoration. It was a place of healing, a church, or ministry; a teaching ministry, a training center, and preparation for ministry, career, or life's work.
- The babies wound on his head, with his scalp split in two, could represent the head of the Church; Paul described the Church as Christ's body.
- The wound meant there'd been a split: people were going to leave, but some would stay.
- The stitches represented the disjointed being put back together. The ones that were left would be joined together again with those who stayed. I knew the Lord had a big plan ahead.

There were many things happening in our personal and business lives, and in our church family.

On October 20, 2013, the Lord led me to read Isaiah chapter 6, which is Isaiah's great commission. His vision was his commission to be God's messenger to his people.

"Isaiah was given a difficult mission. He had to tell people who believed they were blessed by God that instead God was going to destroy them because of their disobedience. Isaiah's lofty view of God gives us a sense of God's greatness, mystery, and power. Isaiah's example of recognizing his sinfulness before God encourages us to confess our sin. His picture of forgiveness reminds us that we, too, are forgiven. When we recognize how great our God is, how sinful we are, and the extent of God's forgiveness, we receive power to do his work. The more clearly Isaiah saw God, the more aware Isaiah became of his own powerlessness and inadequacy to do anything of lasting value without God, but he was willing to be God's spokesman. When God calls, would you also say, 'Here am I. Send me?'" (From the footnotes in the NIV version regarding Isaiah 6:5-8)

The Lord asked if we were willing to choose the rough road ahead to accomplish His greater plan. Were we willing to be used of God for a great purpose, no matter the cost? At that moment I was willing to do anything to see what God had for us, except give up the lives of our boys.

October 29, 2013—another dream. The Lord showed me many things. First, He assured me that, no matter what, He was with me. I had a weakness in my life. I needed to keep seeking Him for that revelation. The family may not believe or come alongside me, but I was not to worry because soon I would have my gifts, and He was preparing me to impart these gifts to others.

I was to submit everything to Him, to trust Him, and to rid myself of self-reliance. People would not have to look for my gifts; He would present them to others and for others. He would equip and prepare me for His special plan. He would give me confidence in my relationships with others, and I would totally submit to the authority of the Holy Spirit.

I would be involved in a healing ministry, exercise spiritual gifts, and worship. I would struggle with my adversary, the devil, who is out to steal, kill, and destroy. I was to relinquish all control. The Lord was releasing me.

He was instructing me to allow His strength to displace my stubborn behavior. I am covered under spiritual authority, deeply rooted in Christ, and no one can take my Lord from me. He is my security.

On October 31, 2013—yet another dream. The Lord showed me the compassion I have for others. My love for others would enable me to help them be delivered from the enemy's grip. Then He warned there would be authority figures who would try to tempt, seduce, deceive, and lure me, but I was to remember that the demonic realm has no control over me. I stand in the authority and under the spiritual authority of Christ and His angels. The Lord once again showed me that I am under His protection.

As I sought God more and more every day, the boys' health continued to deteriorate. On November 1, 2013, my mom requested my help decorating her Christmas tree. She paid $100. I felt it was right to help my mother, and for her to bless us. Work was slow, and we certainly needed the money.

On Sunday, November 2, 2013, I rose early and ran to the corner store to buy some cream for my morning coffee. As I paid with my debit card, I took an extra $20 out in case the kids wanted something to eat at the church. This was unusual for me. I rarely ever withdraw cash.

We left for church, and stopped at the gas station to buy gum.

When Darin ran into the store, the Lord told me that the hundred-dollar bill in my pocket was for somebody at church.

In my heart, I told Him, "I will obey, I will obey."

During the worship portion of the service I began to struggle. I asked Him if He was sure I was to give the $100, or perhaps He meant the $20. He assured me that it was the $100 bill. Once again, I said, "I will obey."

So, as I looked around the room, the Lord showed me the young lady to whom I was to give the money. As I did, I'm not sure who was blessed most—her or me. The Lord gave me peace and joy as a result of obedience.

Exactly four weeks later, I found out that my cousin, Stephanie had conducted a fundraiser for us. She sold stuffed monkeys to people who then donated them back to her so we could bring them to the terminal wing at the hospital where Cameron and Caden always stayed. It was amazing. Not only did we have the joy of giving them as Christmas gifts to the children, but my cousin raised $1,000 for my family. That was ten times the amount I had given out of obedience. Then she took me shopping for gifts for my children.

Isn't it remarkable how our gracious God shows His love to us when we obey Him? Sometimes it is in a monetary gift, and sometimes it is in another form, but our Father God only wants the best for us.

I could not and would not have given that gift had I not been in intimate relationship with the Father. When we are rightly related to the Lord, we are able to hear His voice clearer than the enemy's voice. So press on, get into your relationship with the Lord, and see what He has for you. The joy I felt, and still feel today, cannot be bought nor taken from me. That kind of joy only comes from the Father.

On November 3, 2013 I wrote in my book that I was divinely inspired by the Holy Spirit that we should go out. In 1 Corinthians 1:4 Paul says, *"I always thank God for you because of his grace given you in Christ Jesus."* The Lord is saying our "grace gifts" are given to us to use. We are to be wise, and to receive constructive criticism with grace. We are also to offer critiques with grace. We are to affirm what God has done in others before we offer correction. And we are to always offer correction with the same grace God has shown to us.

On November 4, 2013, Riley had a dream. She was beginning to receive revelation and direction from the Lord. She was warned that she would have friends who are full of poison. She was encouraged to hang out with those who encouraged her toward the Lord, not those who will bring her into ruin. The Lord was warning all of us to be alert and cautious about those we allow to influence us because the enemy is always out to steal kill and destroy.

We all have victory in Christ, overcoming the curse, and in spiritual warfare. We can enjoy intimacy, peace, and covenant with the Father. You see, as Darin and I increased in worship and prayer, the blessings of the Father ran over onto our children. This is why it is so important to commune with the Father continually throughout the day.

On November 9, 2013, Darin was led to read Joshua 8:6: *"They will pursue us until we have lured them away from the city, for they will say, they are running away from us as they did before.' So when we flee from them, you are to rise up from ambush and take the city. The Lord your God will give it into your hand. When you have taken the city, set it on fire. Do what the Lord has commanded. See to it; you have my orders."*

We believe this word is an encouragement for all believers to depend on God with absolute obedience, trusting Him for the victory He has promised.

The Lord says He will send us signs in the heavens and on earth. The Lord will even use earthly signs to communicate with us. There is not one thing that surprises God. "Oops" is not a word in heaven's vocabulary.

On November 15, 2013, at 3:00 in the afternoon, there was a large buck in our driveway. In our neighborhood there are only twelve to twenty feet between houses—not exactly a wildlife refuge.

We have begun to tune our ears to what the Lord is showing us and telling us. We believe this sighting was a sign from the Lord, symbolic of our walk with, our dependence on, and pursuit of God. As for 3:00, the number three represents strength, obedience, the Godhead, and divine fullness. We interpreted it as the Lord telling us He was pleased with our obedience.

We began to log every dream and, through prayer and Scripture research, look for what the Lord is telling us. The Lord speaks to each of us in unique ways. Our family loves to sit and share with one another.

On November 17, 2013, at 5:30 a.m., Caden came into our bedroom, having had a bad dream. He comes to our room when he has dreams because he wants us to help him interpret them. I asked him to describe the dream. He said it was all black-and-white, like an old-time movie. In the dream, our house was called the safe house. Marching around the outside of our house were lots of soldiers with swords, and with them were wolves. He was scared at first, until Darin told him not to fear. Caden said Darin answered the door. The soldiers could not come in, but they told Darin they had come to warn us that the war had begun, and we were to prepare to fight. Then Caden woke up.

We believe that the black-and-white was the Lord telling us we need to be either hot or cold, there is no in between. In Revelation 3:15-16 the Lord says, *"I know you inside and out, and find little to my liking. You are not cold, you are not hot—far better to be either cold or hot! You're stale. You're stagnant. You make me want to vomit."* The Father wants us all, and He wants all of us. We are either all for Christ, or we aren't for him at all. Many soldiers, represents maturity, being fully prepared, service, and judgment (Joshua 3:3-4; Ephesians 4:13; and 1 Samuel 17:5). Soldiers represent messengers, authority, angelic presence, protection in answer to prayer (Revelation 12:7, 10). The swords in the soldiers' hands represent the Word of God, equipped, and prepared (Revelation 6:4). The wolves among the soldiers could mean two things: They could represent predators, or they could mean strength, agility, or leadership (Jeremiah 5:6). Our house represents a place of security, thus the "Safe House".

On January 2, 2014, I was diagnosed with skin cancer. Darin and I prayed and discussed what we would do. The

Lord said, "Do not fear. I am your insurance plan. Have faith in me, and I will heal you." Within three weeks, my skin cancer was gone.

Remember, faith and fear cannot coexist. Faith in the Lord is the opposite of doubt and fear. We cannot embrace both.

On January 11, 2014, a local pastor prophesied that there would be a great outpouring of the Holy Spirit that year, and that we must know God's Word, be filled with the Holy Spirit to the overflowing, pray earnestly, and allow the Lord to use us.

On January 12, 2014, in another of my dreams, the Lord revealed that we were entering into a time of spiritual warfare. Our "old self" was gone, and we would no longer be defined by our sin. We would be clothed with His righteousness and filled with His Spirit. He told us the enemy was on the prowl, and we were to dwell in total unity with Christ because He was making us new, giving us a fresh start. In His perfect timing, He would release us. So we were to position ourselves to receive and remain faithful to what He would be telling us (Genesis 1:1, 5; 8:13; Matthew 6:33). The Lord was going to release His fullness of ministry upon us and complete the work He had begun. Then the Lord led me to read Genesis 1:20, 23; Leviticus 27:31; Matthew 25:2; and 1 Samuel 17:40.

Cameron's and Caden's conditions had not improved, but had grown increasingly worse. We sought God even more through fasting and prayer.

On January 16, 2014, I had another dream: Darin and I were in a bedroom—apparently ours. It had a small bed and two brown couches. I kept trying to get the window air conditioner to fit right in the window. I looked in the closet, and saw that it had a good bright light, so I pulled the string to turn out the light. My thought was "yes" to the couches, because now our friends could visit and be comfortable in our space. I cleaned and put all things in order. Right before I awoke, the Lord said that we would have an apostolic manifestation in our family.

Here was my interpretation:

- Darin represented my authority.
- The bedroom and the bed represented salvation, meditation, peace, rest, and intimacy.
- The two couches represented unity, strength, discernment, union, agreement, and marriage.
- Brown was a representation of our flesh. We're born again, we have repented, we have new life and renewed minds.
- The window represented revelation, the opening of a promise, the truth, heavenly favor, prophecy, understanding, hope, and redemption.
- The air conditioner was a machine which represented work, motion, or success; productivity in motion, making things happen; a role to play, unity.
- The closet represented an inner place, personal, private, prayer, and sanctuary.
- The light represented power and illumination, instantaneous miracle, revelation, knowledge, and the ability to see.

The Lord showed us on January 16th that in our inner place He is all powerful He is going to do instantaneous miracles, we will be very productive and working in unity together and there is an opening of a promise that He had made many years before.

On the morning of January 21, 2014, the cancer the Lord had promised to remove fell off, confirming His faithfulness. That evening at *The Glory Conference* in Rochelle, Illinois, Pastor John Kilpatrick spoke on the story of Jacob, Rachel, and Leah. We have to be fruitful with Leah before God gives us Rachel. Their children's names are significant: Rubin means gifts are given, Simeon means God has heard, Levi means joined to one, Judah means praise. Jacob symbolizes us, and Rachel symbolizes our vision. Leah symbolizes everything we do not want, the places we do not want to go, and our bad circumstances.

During prayer time the Lord had told me that I had to bring all my family to a meeting. I was praying and asking the Lord for a miracle, because the last meeting was on the 22nd, a Wednesday, but we had an appointment Wednesday evening and could not make that meeting. Within five minutes of me asking, the pastor stood and said the Lord told him to extend the meetings through Thursday. That was my miracle; I knew the Lord wanted our family to be there, there was some kind of urgency in the Lord's voice.

On Wednesday I prayed for another miracle, that Darin would also hear from the Lord. He listened to me, and the Lord touched his heart, and he knew we were supposed to go to the last meeting. So I prayed for another miracle: the meetings lasted very late, but my kids had school and homework. I needed the Lord to do something. He did.

School was canceled on Thursday, and had a late start on Friday.

Wednesday night, we took Caden and Cameron for prayer counseling at Wellsprings in Rock Island, Illinois. During that powerful time of ministry, the Lord spoke to Cameron through believers with the gift of discernment (1 Corinthians 12). The following is one letter Cameron received:

> *"Cameron today is the day you choose to be set free and you will be. I fulfill the promise I will never let you down and if you are with me, I will be with you forever and when you call me, I will have an answer for you if you trust me and believe in me. I will be there for you I am your God. I am the great I AM. I know it all. I know your worries; give them to me, I know your fears; give them to me. I make things happen because I am God. You are my beloved son, Cameron, I love you, my precious son; I love you so much. Tonight I want you to be very upfront and honest with your team as I want to free you from these things that you are currently or have struggled with. I want to bring healing to those areas so they will not be a struggle anymore. I want you to bring all of these things that are difficult in your life as once they are exposed and brought out in the open, then we can get rid of them for you. I want your life to be easier on a daily basis, not difficult, so trust me tonight my son, trust me as I want you to leave here freer than you ever have felt before. There were things, actually gifts that were stolen from you by the enemy and I want to restore them back to you. You are a great kid and I am so proud of you for being here*

today. Your smile is a creation of mine and it was designed to light up a room, to show others love by your little grin. You are a precious boy I created, and I want to get closer to you. Cameron, I want to become your best friend. A best friend is someone you talk to daily, confide in, trust in and love dearly. I want to be there for you, and want you to pray to me when things are difficult, when you're having a great day, and, actually, any time day and night. I will be here for you 24 hours a day, seven days a week, every minute of the day. Come to me and praise me, worship me, pray to me, talk to me, draw closer to me and as you draw closer to me, I will draw closer to you. Love your Abba father your best friend."

Here's a word of knowledge for Caden from one of the gifted people in his group:

"I see in Caden a gift of listening and waiting in stillness on the Lord, obeying. He is an obedient boy, a thinker, who likes to tinker and figure things out; to build, tear down, and build again. A young man with a soft heart, moldable, pliable; whose heart will conform to the Lord's heart. I see a breaking down and a building up; a lover of the Lord, a servant, a strong survivor, yet a quiet warrior for the Lord. The Lord will bless him with wisdom, understanding, and godly counsel."

Here's a letter from the Lord to Caden:
"Dear Caden, my son, you are a joy to me. I am so proud of you when you have to take care of your body. You are a very brave

boy. Caden, remember always that I am always, always by your side. I am your friend and protector. I love you, Caden! Your father in heaven."

Here is another letter to Caden:

"My precious son, Caden, you are so dear to me. I love you with all my heart. I am here with you tonight. I am with you always. I know your fears, I know you're suffering, I want nothing but the best for you my dear child. Let me guide your steps tonight, I am your protector. Do not fear, for I am with you. You are my son whom I am so proud of. Keep learning all about me Caden. I will show you who I am, your heavenly father God. I love you."

Caden's last letter:

"Caden, my beloved child, I love you so much. You're such a blessing and I am proud of you. When you feel weak and feel like you are alone, don't give up. I will give you all the strength you need. What may seem like a weakness is strength in disguise. Don't be afraid, for I am always with you. Be strong and courageous; I am your strong tower and protector. I have such great plans for your life, so much more. You need not to let your situation stop you. I have created you to be a great warrior for me. I have not given you a spirit of fear, but of power; trust in me and keep your eyes on me. Be strong and courageous! Your loving and mighty father."

The Lord had told me that, in order for our children to receive on January 23, 2014, my boys had to be delivered from whatever demonic spirits were attached to them. And on January 22, 2013, they were set free from the demons that were taunting them and stealing from them. Cameron saw the demons leaving his body. That night, he slept the best he had slept in a long time. That was an awesome breakthrough.

On January 23, 2014, at 2 o'clock in the afternoon, the nurse from the Florida hospital called me. She wanted to know what we were doing with the boys, because all of Cameron's labs were normal for the first time. I shared with her about the oils I was using and that Cameron had been off of the iron since the first week of December.

Later that evening, we returned to Rochelle, Illinois, to *The Glory Conference* where Pastor Stephen Strader from Lakeland, Florida, spoke.

After the service there was a time of prayer. As I prayed, I experienced sudden heat from my feet through my head and out my hands. About that time the pastor told anybody who felt the move of the Holy Spirit to come forward. I did. There were only about four people up front.

As I continued to pray in submission to the Holy Spirit, the Lord told me to give Him my all—total control of every area of my life. Then the pastor came over to pray for me. The spirit of the Lord was all over me. I could no longer stand, and I went down. As I lay on the floor, the Lord ministered to me. He cleaned out all the areas in my life to make room for more of Him.

As I was giving Him control of everything, every area, every need, and every fear, everything, I opened my eyes and realized I could not get up. There were people everywhere—standing and on the floor. There seemed to be hundreds. I must have been out for a while. I had never experienced the Father in that way.

As I looked around, thinking I needed to get Darin's attention to help me, the Father said, "I am not finished with you."

So I asked the Lord what I was not understanding. Then I looked up and saw Darin at my head, and looked down and saw Madison at my feet, both praying and seeking the Lord.

As I lay in the Lord's presence, He said, "I want your boys." I told Him, I couldn't do it anymore, and whatever He wanted to do, either heal them or take them, I would release them to Him. I knew His plan was best for my boys and for me. I told Him I would praise Him reguardless of what happened. At that moment, the Lord replied, "Now that you have released control, go get your boys because I'm going to heal them tonight."

People were moving toward the front to be healed. In awe, I gathered my senses and went to go get my boys. The pastor announced we should give a praise offering to the Lord. Madison had received the filling of the Holy Spirit, His anointing, and her prayer language.

Darin and I and the boys stood by the front row of chairs, overwhelmed by what the Lord had done with our daughter. The Father nudged me to get prayer for the boys, so we went to a pastor we knew. I only told him that the Lord wanted our boys to get prayer tonight.

Cameron was being ministered to by Glenn and Warren Dunlop, two pastors from Bellfast, Ireland, and we stood with Caden. When pastor Wayne Wiersema finished praying for Caden, he said the Lord told him the boys were going to be healed that night. I was so overwhelmed. This was confirmation of the same word I received.

When Cameron finished receiving ministry, he returned and stood beside us. We could hardly stand up. The Lord was doing "spiritual surgery" on both Darin and me, and visible surgery on our children. Our God is amazing.

As we stood in the front of the first row of chairs, we were in awe. We had been waiting for this day. Then the pastor once again announced that Madison had received the healing anointing that had been on Kathryn Kuhlman, and that we all needed to give the Lord another praise shout. If anyone needed healing, come up, because Madison's hands were on fire with the Lord's anointing.

The pastor took Madison to the other side of the stage because the Lord's glory was hovering on that side. We immediately took the two boys to receive prayer from her. This pastor had never met us, he did not know we were related to Madison. I stood with Cameron in front of me and with Caden beside me, facing Madison and the Pastor, and Darin stood behind Madison.

The pastor took her hand and put it on Cameron's head. As Madison prayed for Cameron, the pastor asked me about Caden. I lifted up Caden's shirt and showed him the feeding tube, and explained that our two boys had a rare liver disease, but that Madison was our daughter.

The pastor was so excited. Darin and I were so overwhelmed by the Spirit of God and what was manifesting upon us, that we fell to the floor again. The pastor once again turned up the microphone and announced this miracle, that the Lord not only was healing our boys, but that He chose to use their sister, and he encouraged the congregation to give praise to Father God for what He was doing.

This moment was and will always be one of the greatest moments of my life. When Madison finished praying for Cameron and Caden, Cameron was excited. He said he felt the liver disease leave his body.

The pastor then took Madison around to the people who raised their hands for healing. He and she walked through the crowd, and people were healed and fell down in the Lord's presence. This went on and on. There was a line of people in chairs in the front row, sitting. Some were crippled and had bones that were disjointed. Madison went to pray for one woman, and the pastor told Madison the Lord wanted her to open her eyes and watch how He was going to use her. When Madison prayed, the woman's bones began to move into place right before her eyes.

Darin was watching, the pastor was watching, the people all around were watching. The bones shifted into place right in Madison's hands as she prayed. The pastor then instructed the lady to get up and run. *She did!*

Our God is good. The miracles increased our faith, and others' faith also. We went home knowing the glory of God fell upon us, and we were excited for what He would do next.

The next day, Friday, January 24th, 2014, I woke up, and the Lord said, "I want you to call three elders, the associate pastor, and the senior pastor of your church to testify what I have done."

I did, and shared the whole story. The elders came over for prayer and received, in part, what we had received.

This was the first time I had ever felt my hands get oily. The elder explained to me what that was, and I was amazed. My hands were on fire; not only did I feel the heat, but others did also. The heat seemed to come out of me and transfer to these elders and their wives. It was like living in a heavenly dream. I invited them to go back to that church for the evening service, because we were going back.

On Friday, Cameron said he was not going to take anymore cornstarch. I struggled with this decision, because of all of the years of treatment.

When we arrived at the church, one of the prophets, James Fox, and his wife approached us and said the Lord had given him a word the night before:

"When I came up to you last night, the power of God was moving everywhere, and I came up to you and you went down. The Lord spoke to me immediately, and I thought I would get to you later but it never happened. The Lord arranges these things to happen. When you went down, what I saw was this. I saw fire shoot out of you, and I was wondering what God was trying to speak because I didn't know what fire it was. There are lots of differences of fires, God has a lot of variety of fire, but He said the glory is coming out of her. The glory is coming out of her. Okay, so I asked what does that mean. But the idea is going to start flowing through you. The glory is going to start flowing through you, okay? You are going to start seeing physical demonstrations and physical manifestations of the glory starting to flow through you. Now when this starts to happen, it will be for the glory of the Kingdom of God. That's the only thing God does. God does nothing unless it glorifies His Kingdom. Everything revolves around it, and no matter what, it always glorifies His kingdom. So what's going to happen is, you are going to have power in your hands. Your hands are going to start. You are going to start having power in your hands. Now you may feel heat or you may not. You may even see fire on your hands… the idea is that you will know there is going to be glory coming out of your hands. All prophecy is confirmation, and you wait for the

confirmation before you act on it. Now, it will come out of your hands, but it's going to come out of your mouth, too. The glory is going to come out of your mouth to the point that when you speak the word of God towards anything that needs to be taken care of, the glory will shoot out of your mouth and hit it. The Word of the Lord—allow yourself to have the Word in you like never before. Be a student of the Word, and be a student of the Bible. Get the Word in you so, when you speak, the Word comes out of you. Now with this is coming an entire ministry of deliverance. You need to learn all there is about deliverance. It's a fun ministry. Most people are scared of it, and most people don't understand it. But it's fun once you understand there is no fear involved. Okay? Fear cannot be involved. If fear is there, they have control. So you can't allow fear to come in, and the spirit of the Lord will make sure, the Holy Spirit will make sure you have no fear. He's going to start bringing people to you for this problem, on the street. This next move of God is not going to be in the buildings. Jesus did very little in the buildings, and most all of His ministry was outside on the streets. Now the next thing—Darin, this is where you come involved—Korene, he is your covering. This is the way it is set up: so, he is your covering, and he is going to be able to help you understand what is going on. God is going to give him wisdom to help guide you. And in that the two of you are going to make a good team, because you have a strong relationship right now and, with that strong relationship, you are going to be a dynamic duo for the Lord."

72

That word has come to pass!

We decided to focus on what the Lord had done and wanted to do. We stopped watching television, and consecrated our free time to studying the Word. It's amazing what the Lord does when we give Him all control and let Him lead us.

We had received the results of the blood tests for both boys. Cameron's blood values were all normal, and Caden's were much improved but not yet perfect. Cameron stopped all daily treatment, and we continued to test him every three hours. His blood values were normal.

Caden's blood values were normal, but we continued with his treatment.

I have to testify about Caden. In the past, he would be unable to walk or even get up without his treatment. If his ketones were above 0.5, we would have to take him to the ER because the toxic levels would cause him to slip into unconsciousness.

One morning, he woke up sick with symptoms. I tested him. His sugars were low at sixty-four, and his ketones were at a toxic level of 1.1. I was anxious, but Caden was walking around, telling me he wanted to eat and that he would be better. Within thirty minutes, his blood values were all normal.

The Lord told me to remember what He had done. Even though Cameron's healing came instantly and Caden's was progressive did not mean He did not heal Caden.

I still had a lot to learn. I talked with Madison about the boys' blood levels and she, with the Father's wisdom said, "Mom, it is okay. The Lord wants us to be able to minister to people of both healings." She was encouraging, as if the Lord already showed her. That is why the Lord tells us to have that childlike faith and innocence.

In February 2014, Cameron stopped his nightly feedings, and his blood values remained normal. Caden has been admitted into the hospital only one time in nine months for high fever and dehydration. His blood values remain stable, and the Lord keeps showing His faithfulness to His promise of healing Caden. We had another appointment with the specialist in Iowa City in early March, and told the specialist about the healings. Well, he may not have agreed with us, but he could not refute it. All of Cameron's labs were normal, his liver and spleen were normal size and had normal function. Caden's liver and spleen were normal size and function, and all of his blood values were all normal.

This was truly a miracle from our God. Now was the time to share what the Lord had done. Every chance we had, we would testify to what the Lord had done and what He is continually doing.

In early March, my dad came by to see how things were going. He was standing funny, and I asked him what was wrong. He said that he did something to his back, and it had been hurting him for weeks. I had never prayed for my dad before, but stepped out and told the kids we were going to pray for grandpa. He was all for it, so we all laid our hands on him and prayed for healing and no more pain.

A couple weeks later, he had told me his back stopped hurting the moment he walked out my door that day, and every time I see him he says his back still doesn't hurt. I asked if he believed in that miracle, and he said yes. Now, that is a testimony. There are many more miracles that have happened in our home. These testimonies have grown our faith. Our children are bold for Jesus—they pray first and ask questions later. I give God all the glory.

In April I was praying, and the Lord said that it was time to open up our home to pray for people. The Word says when we receive from the Lord, we are to give what we receive. The Lord had been telling me this for a couple of years. I finally believed it was time. I asked the Lord to name it and set a day. He said it would be called SHOPP—Safe House of Prayer & Praise—and it would be on Tuesday evenings so it does not interfere with other church events. We opened up our home, and the Lord has done miracle after miracle.

As I gave our testimony to people, I told everyone that we are on the Jesus train. Now, when I say *train,* I mean the train of His robe. The father said that there is room for everyone, but we are not to get off to get people on the train. That spoke to me. I know many people who would rather keep living the way they are because it's comfortable. Unless you sacrifice everything and follow Jesus, you are never going to be totally comfortable. If you will give Him control, watch and see what He does for you.

We continue to attend our home church, Calvary Lighthouse in Rochelle, Illinois, and other spirit-filled churches when ours is not meeting. We are hungry for more of Jesus. We have access to all He has, we just haven't received it all yet. It is all a sacrifice, but it is worth it.

Every time we drive the ninety minutes to church, the Lord shows us more love and revelation and direction. We have received major acceleration in all our gifts. The Lord continues to speak to me through my dreams, and now to my whole family, also. I have received the husband the Lord promised me when I was ten years old—a bold man of the Lord who speaks about Jesus all the time—and my kids are all on fire for the Lord.

As the year went on, the Lord spoke to me about homeschooling the next year to be more flexible in the ministry He has for us. He dropped this into my spirit on a Monday, and by Friday He had it all worked out. There was a teacher to oversee the curriculum, the curriculum was chosen, Darin was all for it, and all the kids were in agreement to be homeschooled.

Later that Friday, we again went to Calvary Lighthouse Church. They were having a celebration of all the prodigals coming home to Jesus. We sat with Mr. and Mrs. Fox. Mr. Fox asked, "So, what is the word for the day?" I told them what the Lord had done that week, directing us to homeschool the next school year. He told me the Lord was waiting for us to be more fluid, not just flexible, in our schedule for the ministry. Darin and I just sat there in shock. We haven't only heard from the Lord and obeyed, but the word of the Lord was confirmed that very day.

Let's talk about *acceleration*. The Lord had told many of these apostles, prophets, evangelists, pastors, and teachers the word for the year was *acceleration*: there would be an acceleration of the outpouring of the Holy Spirit upon His people. I testify to that on our family's behalf.

From January to April 2014, the Lord had given all of our household new revelation. The Lord showed Madison that we will be ministering as a family to others. Prophetic words came, one after another, about ministering to others.

On May 27th, 2014, the Lord told me that our ministry will be like a large oak tree, deeply rooted, strong. It will bear much fruit, and it will withstand opposition. It is planted by the living water flowing from the Father.

Later that week, the Lord gave us visions of what was going to happen. I am amazed at His voice sometimes. Every day I ask for an answer or for direction, and He always reveals something, not always does it look like I think it should but He knows what is best for me.

The Lord wants to use everyone who is willing to be His vessel. Isaiah 6:1-8 talks about being that willing vessel, used for the Lord. 2 Timothy 2:21 says, *"If a man cleanses himself from the latter, he will be an instrument for noble purposes, made holy, useful to the Master and prepared to do any good work."* The Lord wants to use anyone willing to be used by Him for His Glory. This is only the beginning.

The Lord says in Ephesians 3:20 that *"now to him who is able to do immeasurably more than all we ask or imagine, according to His power that is at work within us."* The Lord is saying the Word and the power of the Lord are amazing; but that together, they are perfection.

The Lord has a plan and purpose for your life, if you ask the Lord Jesus Christ into your heart, and confess Him as Lord and Savior of your life. Just receive all He has for you. Our purpose in life is to share Jesus with everyone. It has become easier for our family because we have positioned ourselves and surrounded ourselves with like-minded believers.

As I explained before, our boys had many hospital visits and specialist monitoring their progress every month, and in February 2014 the boy's labs were completely normal. This caused many questions from the doctors. They started to watch us very carefully. They would run the labs as scheduled, and the results would always come back normal. Caden went off his cornstarch, at his request, because he knew he was healed. I still tested his blood values every three hours for weeks.

We then went to the Children's Hospital again to run all the lab work. In one week all of their lab results were mailed to me, and wept as I read them. *They were normal.* I even called the specialist, and it was confirmed: all normal. The Lord showed me that He is always faithful and His promises always come to pass. He told me to never forget what He had done, and now I keep a copy of those normal lab results in my Bible.

This new life we have been given is amazing, but the enemy is still the father of lies. Any time I feel or start to think that the boys are not healed, I look at those lab results and the Lord gives me peace from the top of my head to the bottom of my feet. I know they are healed, praise the Lord.

One of our last visits to the Children's Hospital was in October 2014. This was a confirming visit for me. We had to take Cameron and Caden for their regular checkups and lab work. The doctor also had to change Caden's feeding tube, necessary for one bedtime feeding of Glycosade. Before he was healed, Caden did not eat much and his skeletal muscles were depleted of proteins. This feeding allows his muscles to continue to grow, and helps him gain his appetite back after years of not eating much.

When he has gained the muscle mass needed, his feeding tube will be removed. One of the specialists came in to evaluate our visit, and to look at the boys' lab test results. Cameron answered all of the doctor's questions. He told of his healing. This doctor had the most confused look on her face as Cameron explained in detail what had happened, and Caden added that he had been healed also and no longer takes cornstarch. She looked at me in disbelief, and then looked at Darin, until we confirmed what the boys had said was, in fact, true.

Then the doctor suddenly asked me where this took place, who was in charge, in what town, and what was the name of the pastor. She even wrote it down in her notes. About this time, another specialist came in. This one had been taking care of our boys for a couple years, and listened intently to our conversation. When we finished testifying, both specialists looked at the computer at both boys' lab results, past and present, along with growth charts. They also measured their livers and spleens. Now both specialists began to ask questions. We were so excited to share what the Lord had done that our excitement hit one of the doctors, and she suddenly asked if we could pray for her healing, because she was diabetic.

We agreed, and the other specialist suddenly realized that the questions he was asking were probably not allowed by hospital policy, and he said he could not inquire any further about this healing. Although he did not ask any more questions, he did request a copy of this book, and then released the boy's until next year because all of their labs were normal. They had grown to an average size for their age, and their livers and spleens were now normal in size.

The doctors left this visit knowing about Jesus, and seeing with their very own eyes a miracle that had taken place. One of the doctors even requested her own miracle. Remember, nothing is too big for our God.

Our lives have changed forever. A prophet had told us that going to Florida to see Dr. Weinstein was not a waste of time. The Lord had taught us to persevere. We are to stand with God and stand on His promises. I believe you must let the Holy Spirit come upon you, let Him work in you and through you. Once you begin to participate with the Holy Spirit, you take the limits off of what can be done through you. Luke 1:37says, *"For nothing is impossible with God."* The divine connection lifts all limitations. The Holy Spirit wants to empower you to do all things through Christ. We all need to give God the opportunity to manifest in our lives, so communicate with the Father through the Holy Spirit without ceasing.

Faith will change the atmosphere around you. We have been transformed into the likeness of Jesus Christ. We learn through spending as much time as we possibly can with the Lord and in His word, and we will become a different type of people, hungry for more of the Lord. We want to hear Him more clearly, obey Him without delay, and share Him with as many people as we can.

We need to carry God's climate. This climate draws people who hunger for the anointing of the Father.

Our family's faith has increased because of our boys' healings, but that is just the beginning. The Bible says in Ephesians 4:7-8, 11-13,

> *"But to each one of us grace is given as Christ apportioned it. This is why it says: 'When he ascended on high, he led captives in his train and gave gifts to men.' It was he who gave some to be apostles, some to be prophets, some to be evangelists,*

and some to be pastors and teachers, to prepare God's people for works of service, so that the body of Christ may be built up until we all reach unity in faith and in the knowledge of the Son of God and become mature, attaining to the whole measure of the fullness of Christ."

As we prepare ourselves and look for opportunities to serve others, God will show them to us. Then, as we begin to recognize our gifts, we will be able to be used by the Lord to strengthen and encourage others. Everyone has spiritual gifts. 1 Corinthians 12:1-11 explains these gifts and how they are given by the Holy Spirit.

Remember, we are merely human beings who are willing to be used however the Lord wills. The spiritual gifts are given to each person by the Holy Spirit, and are to be used to minister to the needs of the body of believers.

Mark 16:15-18 tells us to go preach the gospel to all creation, and that all who believe and are baptized will be saved. When we pursue the heart of the Father, and persevere until we get our breakthrough, the Lord will come into our situation at the perfect time and fulfill His promises to us.

For thirteen years, this disease was killing Cameron; and, for six years, Caden. Romans 5:2b-5 says, *"And we rejoice in the hope of the glory of God. Not only so, but we rejoice in our sufferings, because we know that suffering produces perseverance; perseverance, character; character, hope. And hope does not disappoint us, because God has poured out his love into our hearts by the Holy Spirit, whom he has given us."*

Hope grows as we learn more about all the things God has for us. It gives us the promise of the future. And God's love fills our lives and gives us the ability to reach out to others. So rejoice in your sufferings—your tests in life become His testimony to others who do not believe. Our story is just one of many, and you also have a story.

As this book comes to an end, I pray that this story will cause an internal fire to ignite and burn inside of you so wherever you go people will see and want what you have. Keep testifying about all that the Lord has done, and continue to seek His face and watch the glory of God manifest, for His presence resides in His glory.

Lord Jesus, I pray in Jesus' Holy name that You go to the person who has read this book. I pray for their salvation. I ask that You send Your ministering angels and healing power upon them. Thank You, Jesus, for all You have done in our lives and for what You are about to do in the lives of others. In Jesus' Holy Name, Amen.

A Sister's Point of View

By Madison Sturtz

Growing up with two brothers who were diagnosed with a rare liver disease called *Glycogen Storage Disease type IX* (GSD), not one of the highlights of my life, slowly turned into something amazing.

It all started with my little brother Cameron. He was only four years old, and he was having very bad sicknesses in the morning. It didn't just happen once or twice, but almost continually. As a seven-year-old little girl, all I saw was Cameron getting more care and affection from my parents, so I became jealous because he received all the attention. Little did I know that he was in pain almost every day and no doctor could tell us what was happening.

I cannot tell you how well my parents handled it. They kept pressing through, searching for answers.

When my brother was four, my little sister, Riley was on the way, so not only did my parents have to deal with my brother being sick all the time, but also a baby girl on the way. To be honest, I felt lost, and I didn't get very much attention, so I faked being sick a couple of times. Today, I know my parents were trying hard to give me every little bit of their attention.

Riley arrived, and we tried to move on. Mom tried to tell the doctors that there was something else wrong, and doctors are very intelligent, but they didn't listen at all.

It was traumatizing to see my little brother in the hospital, hooked up to wires, and to see his face so fair and pure and innocent, wondering why he deserved this.

When Caden, my other little brother was born, everything was going well until he also became sick, much worse than Cameron. Both of my brothers would get up in the morning not knowing if they would have symptoms. They would both get so sick they couldn't walk and would barely even eat. They just lay there like puppets on strings, all hooked up to IVs, puking up everything they ate.

Even when I would get jealous, I was never angry at them, but at the circumstances, wondering what was going to happen next.

Then, after going from one doctor to the next, we were sent to a specialist down in Florida. Finally, we had some hope. Then we were told the most terrible news anyone could receive: both boys had a rare liver disease and wouldn't live much past thirteen.

My first thoughts were, "How could this happen? When did they get this? How could we fix it?" My heart was broken, and anger burned inside me.

The doctor said he would run some more tests, and I thought, "Great, another doctor who doesn't know anything." But he later told us there are other kids out there with the same disease, and corn starch could stabilize my brothers' blood sugars and ketones.

They started to get better, never one hundred percent, but better, than they were before. We finally started to see a change and live a little more normal life. We had more family time. Even though the boys were not totally normal and still got sick, it seemed they were getting better, and we had a fighting chance.

We then started to try to help the other kids with the same or similar diseases, and we put on fundraisers to raise money for more research.

During all of this we stayed strong in the Lord and never gave up. The strongest person in all of this was my mom; she did everything. She never gave up even when all of us wanted to, and she knew something else was wrong and found out the answer. She prayed and stayed strong.

We visited a friend's church, and after that we went to a church in Rochelle, Illinois, not really expecting anything. I just sat and listened. And, wow, I thought that this church was crazy and wild, with people falling everywhere and jumping up and down, but when the pastor asked if anyone needed prayer, I went up front. No one knew who I was, but two men asked me if I wanted to be *filled*.

I didn't know what that meant, but I said yes. After they prayed for me, an overwhelming sense of peace and joy came over me.

Then one man asked, "Would you like the gift of tongues?" I said yes. He also said I have a healing anointing upon me, and then he announced to everyone who ever needed healing come up to the front of the church.

Mom came up, and the pastor placed my hands on my brothers' heads. Caden went down. Cameron said the disease left his body, and my mom wept with joy. Then she told the pastor that I was their sister, and he smiled and was very excited. She told him some of what had happened with the boys, and we all witnessed a miracle that day.

I started to place my hands on people, seeing miracles, I have never seen before, right in front of me.

When we returned home, Mom contacted the doctor, told him what happened, and showed him the boys' blood labs. He said, "Whatever you are doing, keep doing it."

We shared our story with everyone we knew, we were so excited to see what God was doing in our lives. God showed us with that one miracle that He is in control, and now we are searching for Him more and praising Him for what He did. And God is using our story to show others He can change their lives as well.

CPSIA information can be obtained
at www.ICGtesting.com
Printed in the USA
LVOW05s0711130116
470335LV00005B/6/P

9 781312 909274